It's Always Something

Paiton Williams

It's Always Something © 2023

Paiton Williams

All rights reserved.

No part of this publication may be
reproduced, stored in a retrieval system, or
transmitted, in any form or by any means,
electronic, mechanical, photocopying,
recording or otherwise, without the prior
written permission of the presenters.

Paiton Williams asserts the moral right to
be identified as the author of this work.

Presentation by *BookLeaf Publishing*

Web: www.bookleafpub.com

E-mail: info@bookleafpub.com

ISBN: 9789358310276

First edition 2023

To my parents, my sisters, my niece and nephew, my grandparents, my best friend, and my person. I'd be nothing without all of you.

PREFACE

~They asked, "What are you thinking about?"

I said, "Oh nothing."

But what I meant was "everything."~

Hand-Me-Downs

My sister gives her kids a bath
and those hellions trash the whole dang
bathroom.
How?
Toddlers, I guess.

She takes the kids downstairs
and I go in behind her to clean.
Bathtub toys get dried off and put in the basket.
Baby shampoo gets put back on the shelf.
Is this towel clean? - doesn't smell like it.
Throw away the dirty diapers.
Throw away the hair left in the drain.
Throw away the dead plant from last Mother's
Day still sitting in the window.

Then I find something I can't throw away.

A memory.

Jazz

Crimson, clover, midnight
blue,
all different colors,
all matching hues,
And every one of them
pertaining to you.
Like the feeling of
mahogany,
a little weathered, but silky to the touch.
And still very strong.
Like fresh cotton sheets on days like these.
Like the Raven's hidden song.

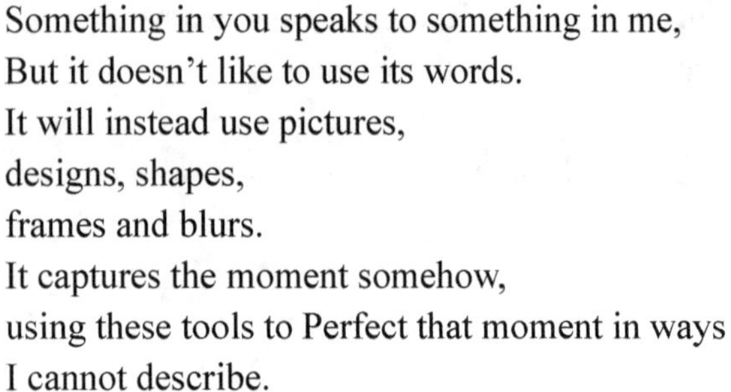

Something in you speaks to something in me,
But it doesn't like to use its words.
It will instead use pictures,
designs, shapes,
frames and blurs.
It captures the moment somehow,
using these tools to Perfect that moment in ways
I cannot describe.

And trust me, I've tried.

Baby Bird

And so the boy,
weeping,
knelt down.
And as he did,
he laid down his sword,
he took off his crown.

To find a jewel,
of more value than men,
To find life,
and,
for it to be here?
To be given, to be taken,
that he could not comprehend.

It was that day he swore,
on all the birds in the sky -
any bird that could fly,
he would weep,
nevermore.

For you see, he knew what was up ahead,
and he knew he could not take it lightly.
But the jewel on the ground
made such a unique sound -
One day,
turned into Nightly.

Sweaters from Sophomore Year

It's Algebra II and I'm terrible at math.
Why does the school even have this class?
The desks were set up in groups, and her name
was Nadine.
It was the first day of class, and she sat to my
right.
Coach Lebanowski was a no B.S. kind of
teacher, and she had just moved from out of
state.
Homework assigned on the first day, and we sat
together at lunch.

Homecoming came and went.
The heart-shaped sticky notes inside her locker.
Football games came and went.
The paint parties and late-night Waffle House
dinners.
Spring break came and went.
The day at the skatepark complaining about the
food truck fries, and then eating a 2nd order.
Finals came and went.
Spending a half day playing uno and drawing in
each other's notebooks.

And she moved out of state.

That was ten years ago,
And I still think we had the coolest matching
sweaters.

House on Fire

Now you're calling me crazy,
but the kitchen is hazy,
the smell of burning eggs
it's staining the air.

And you're calling me lazy,
but we're coming up daisies!
Just don't open the closet,
it'll give you a scare.

Antebellum

So I dug this hole
Six feet down
And I'm sitting on the edge
Just staring at the ground

I dug this hole
Six feet down
And I'm falling off the edge
While my feet dangle down

Protector

He was steady.
Towering.
With such broad shoulders
that look like they used to
hold the weight of
His wings.

Now they carry only
the weight of
His fears.

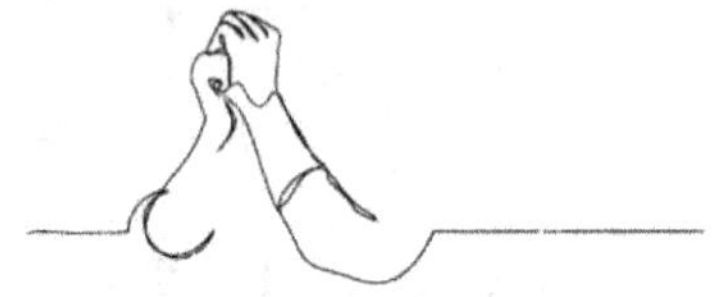

Life is for the Living (from the Dead)

When I die
I do not want a coffin.
I want one of those pods
that decomposes
and turns me into a tree.
That way I can grow.
Grow a strdy trunk to give critters a place to
sleep.
Grow flowing branches to give birds a place to
rest.
Grow bountiful fruits to give weary travelers
new energy.

When I die,
use me for science.
Put me on a slab and
make a diagram of me.
That way we can grow.
Use me to find the cure for the common cold.
Use me to find the reason behind cancer.
Use me to find purpose.

When I die,
I want to keep sustaining life.

26 years, 1 month, 3 weeks.

They say growth happens slowly.
And if you try to speed up the
process, the whole thing could
revert back to where you started.
So, I'm assuming it's like one day
I'll wake up and go, "oh wow, look
how much I've changed!"
Or, are you supposed to notice the
changes along the way?

I want to know what it's like for the caterpillar.
Do their little brains consciously know what
they are going to become?
Required to completely dissolve, on a cellular
level, in order to move on to the next stage of
life.
Isn't that daunting?
Molecules buzzing around in such a tightly
controlled space.
Neurons firing signals across what seems like
galaxies inside that chrysalis.
Oblivious to the construct of time.
To emerge an entirely brand new being,
something beautiful and captivating.
A product of the universe's hard work.
I'd like to think this is my chrysalis.

Whispers

Little secrets turn into Big Secrets,
And Big Secrets outgrow their chains.
Though she may have been a free woman,
Inside a prison, she remained

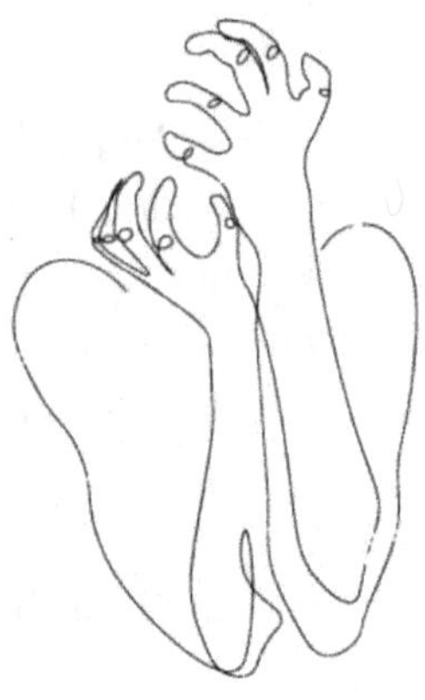

Compromise.

Concede, concede.
No arguing.
No defeating.

Nolo. Concede.

Swallowing your pride doesn't give you
indigestion.

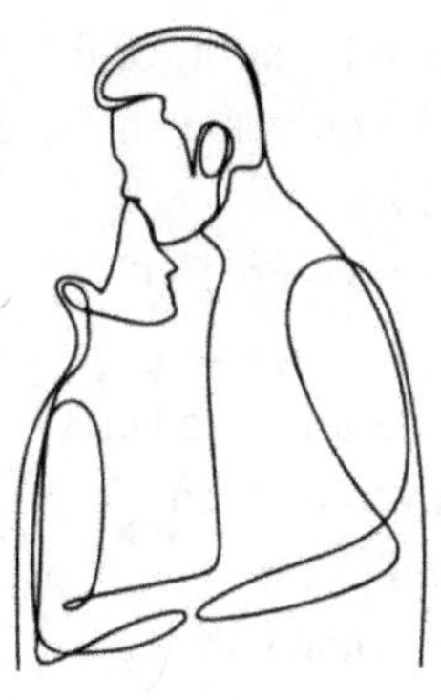

Daily Dose

I read a poem somewhere that said something
like, "the best way to live with regret is to tell
yourself you didn't know better at the time."
That poem was probably written very
eloquently,
probably had multiple verses with colorful
vocabulary.
Probably got some recognition, maybe even the
author won an award for how popular the poem
became.
I can't remember all the words, but I remember
how I felt when I read it for the first time.
Almost like the universe answered a question I
didn't know I had:
"How do I live with regret?"
- I don't.
She doesn't actually live here.
She doesn't even pay rent.
She comes and goes.
She moves in when she needs a place to crash
for a couple hours.
She knows every nook and cranny of this mind.
She blocks the door with her bags.
She paints the walls with self-loathing.
She finds my stash of joy and eats it.

All.
And when she's full and rested, she leaves.
Taking nothing but time on her way out.

But before she comes again,
I think I'll rearrange the furniture.

15

The Simple Things

I have spent hundreds of dollars on cat toys over
the years.
Ones that move or rotate.
Some with lights, or funky laser pointers.
Stuffed ones with catnip inside,
I've given them catnip just straight out of the
bag.

And you know what those little twerps love the
most?
A used plastic straw.

Oh, to spend a day as a cat in the Williams
household.

You and I

I wish you and I were flowers
planted together,
grown in the same field.
Our roots deep in the soil,
grounded, intertwining.
So I could know your touch
ever since the beginning.

I wish you and I were flowers
picked together,
pressed on the same page.
The edges of our petals
overlapping by centimeters.
So I can know your touch
even in the end.

She&Her

They wined and dined
and laughed all night,
candles illuminating each room.

Shadows love to play their tricks -
under the chandelier,
under the table,
under the light of the moon.

What was forbidden,
now to be undone.
Just a stitch in history's loom.

And if one were out,
in the midnight square,
in the span of time -
of misplace and mistrust,
of darkness and lust,
one always has space to make room.

Color Bar

The black stool and the white chair
sat down for a green drink.

But the brown bench got jealous
and turned all shades of pink.

The yellow couch and orange recliner
gave each other a wink,

And the purple velvet casket
Will cost a lot more than you think.

Growing Up.

Inertia demands I keep going.

I won't make your mistakes.

Again.

Pembroke

In the year Pembroke was conceived,
her mother was most certainly pleased.
She joyously shouted and spoke,
"My boy will be named Pembroke!"

In the year Pembroke emerged,
the town's cheers were overheard.
Miles and miles of villagers knew,
that she was the first of many,
the last one of few.

In the year Pembroke came of age,
her mother was filled with intense rage.
For she, her mother that is, wanted a son when
she was born.
Now and forever, she was scorn.

In the year of Pembroke's birthright,
she wandered out into the night.
There she waited patiently,
calling upon a friend named normalcy.

In the year when Pembroke asked,
"Where art thou, my love at last?"
She had long waited all her life,

never knowing she was meant for a wife.

In the year Pembroke aged,
she paid a visit to the mage.
He told her "go on, be free,
for I no longer have use of thee."

In the year that Pembroke died,
she had the brightest blue eyes.
The ones you cannot turn away,
the ones that shown in the darkest of days.

Sunday Nights

The birds chirping
The wind in the trees
The wasps buzzing
The neighbor's dog barking
The cars driving by
The cheers from the football stadium a block
over
The sizzling of steaks
The shouting of video game shooting
The dishes clinking together

The laughter of loved ones.

I Named Her Joy

My youngest cat is a Gemini
through and through.
She loves to be pet
only on her head and butt -
And if you even THINK about the belly,
it's over.
She drools (yes, really).
She does NOT like to be picked up.
She screams for attention at 5:23 AM.

But when she decides it's cuddle time
and I get to look into her golden yellow eyes,
it's like finding her
and falling in love.
All over again.

New Horizons

He said to me tonight
"Thanks for talking to me about this. I really
needed it."

For the first time,
I don't feel afraid of saying what's on my mind,
Unfiltered.

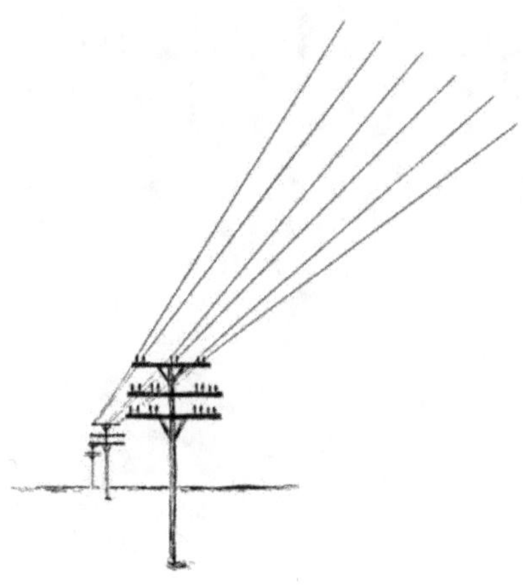

www.ingramcontent.com/pod-product-compliance
Lightning Source LLC
La Vergne TN
LVHW021349200726
843509LV00014B/2754